B55 075 685 8

A Question of History

what happened to a pharaoh's brain?

and other questions about the ANCIENT EGYPTIANS

Tim Cooke

D1341329

WAYLAND
www.waylandbooks.co.uk

First published in Great Britain in 2021
by Wayland

© Hodder and Stoughton, 2021

All rights reserved

Credits:
Editor: Julia Bird
Design and illustrations: Matt Lilly
Cover design: Matt Lilly

ISBN hb 978 1 5263 1492 5
ISBN pb 978 1 5263 1493 2

Printed and bound in China

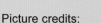

MIX
Paper from
responsible sources
FSC® C104740
FSC
www.fsc.org

Picture credits:

Alamy: Ancient Art & Architecture 27tr; Azoor Photo 24t; Pan Chaoyue/Xinhua 11tl; Chris Deeney 7tl; Eye Ubiquitous 6b; Granger Historical Picture Agency 12bl, 13tc,18l, 23c, 29t; Peter Horee 28t; Interfoto 26t; KGPA Ltd 21b; Prisma Archivo 15b; Science History Images 17t; The Print Collector 13tr. **Dreamstime:** Kguzel 15tl. **Shutterstock**: Juan Aunion 9tr, 19t; Baibaz 22bl; Gurgen Bakkhshetyan 11tc; Zhang Baohuan 11tr; Blue Ice 13br; Nick Brundle 20b; Cholpan 4b; Claudio Divizia 13bl; Dunhill 25b; Khaled ElAdawy 7r; Zbigniew Guzowski 20t; Anton Ivanov 8-9c; jenni.ir 17b; Jsp 22cr; Leshiy985 5b; Dario Lo Presti 13cr; Love Lego 14b; Maeadv front cover, 1, 4t; Jaroslav Moravcik 21t; Morphart Creation 16t; Mountainpix 24b, 27cl; Mountains Hunter 8l; Yakov Oskanov 29b; Scott Rothstein 15c; Jose Ignacio Soto 13c; Lisa Strachan 18r; Punnawit Suwattananun 10br; Eric Valenne/geostory 10bl.

Every effort has been made to clear copyright.
Should there be any inadvertent omission, please apply
to the publisher for rectification

Wayland
An imprint of
Hachette Children's Group
Part of Hodder and Stoughton
Carmelite House
50 Victoria Embankment
London EC4Y 0DZ

An Hachette UK Company
www.hachette.co.uk
www.hachettechildrens.co.uk

Rotherham Libraries	
B55 075 685 8	
PETERS	25-Jan-2022
J932	8.99
CHILD	RTWIC

Contents

Who were the ancient Egyptians?

If you were asked to name an old civilisation, there is a good chance you would think of the ancient Egyptians. Everyone has heard of the pyramids, the pharaohs (rulers) and the mummies.

SO IS THERE ANYTHING LEFT TO LEARN?

ACTUALLY, YES!

Thousands of years

One thing you might not realise about the ancient Egyptians is how long they were around for. Their civilisation began in about 3150 BCE. It lasted until the Romans conquered Egypt in 30 CE.

That's over 3,000 years!

This ancient stone palette is believed to show the joining of Lower and Upper Egypt into one country (see page 5) in around 3150 BCE.

Ancient Egyptian history is divided into three long periods, when the state was generally stable:

the **Old Kingdom**, **Middle Kingdom** and **New Kingdom**. There were also three Intermediate Periods, when rulers competed for power. Oh, and there was also a late period when it came under Greek influence.

Thin but long

Another thing you might not realise about ancient Egypt is its odd shape. Most Egyptians lived in the valley of the River Nile. That meant the country was only about 16 kilometres wide – but almost 1,450 kilometres long! To the east and the west lay bone-dry desert.

Egyptians saw their kingdom as two regions. Upper Egypt was the narrow river valley in the south. Lower Egypt was in the north, where the Nile split into channels, creating a fan-shaped delta.

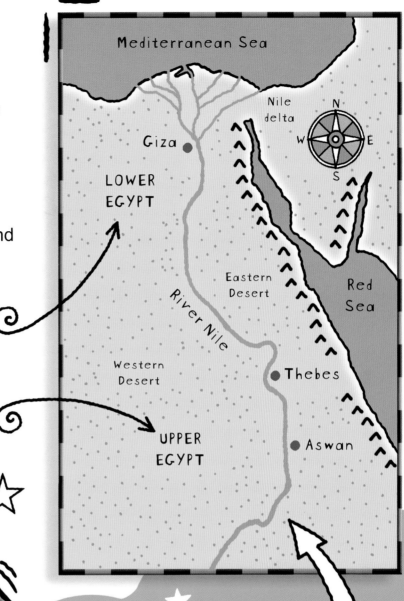

Mediterranean Sea

Nile delta

Giza

LOWER EGYPT

N
W   E
S

Eastern Desert

River Nile

Red Sea

Western Desert

Thebes

UPPER EGYPT

Aswan

Life-giving river

The Nile was at the heart of ancient Egyptian life. It provided:

Irrigation (water) for crops, and a highway for boats. Also, fish for food, reeds for making papyrus, or paper, a site for temples and pyramids...

...AND mud for making bricks!

Because the Nile was vital to everything the ancient Egyptians did, it's a good place to start...

Why did the Egyptians pray for floods?

Most people hate floods. Everything gets wet and soggy. Not the ancient Egyptians! The Egyptians loved it when the Nile overflowed. That was lucky, as it happened for months every year.

ON YOUR MARKS, GET SET... FLOOD!

Black or red?

Egyptians divided their territory into the Black Land and the Red Land. The Black Land, or Kemet, included the delta and the Nile valley. The soil there was dark and full of nutrients for growing crops. The Red Land was the desert to the east and west of the Nile valley. Only miners went there to gather minerals, although it did help to protect Egypt from hostile neighbours.

When the floods ended, farmers used irrigation ditches to water their crops. The floods left behind a layer of fine, rich silt carried down the Nile from the heart of Africa. This silt nourished the soil and helped farmers to grow barley and emmer wheat for food, and flax for oil and for making cloth.

Irrigation ditch

MORE OFFERINGS PLEASE!

Hapi

Keeping Hapi happy

Hapi, the god of the Nile, was also the god of fertility. The Egyptians left him offerings of food and drink to ask him to ensure the Nile would flood at the right time – and not too much.

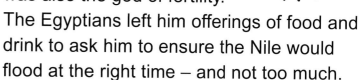

They needed to keep Hapi happy!

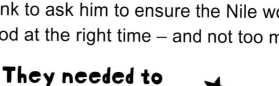

The crops grown in the rich Nile valley allowed Egypt to feed a large population, despite its lack of farmland.

Measuring the Nile

Egyptians predicted the flood depths with nilometers. In other words, holes.

A hole was dug beside the river, with a scale marked on its walls to show the depth of the water in the river. Some nilometers had sets of stone steps inside that measured the water.

I THINK WE'RE WELL AND TRULY FLOODED!

A nilometer in Cairo, Egypt

Which Egyptian pharaoh was actually a woman?

Hatshepsut ruled Egypt from around 1473 to 1458 BCE. There are many statues that show him wearing a kilt and the royal crown, with a muscly body and the false beard worn by all Egyptian pharaohs. The only thing is …

…this ruler was actually a queen!

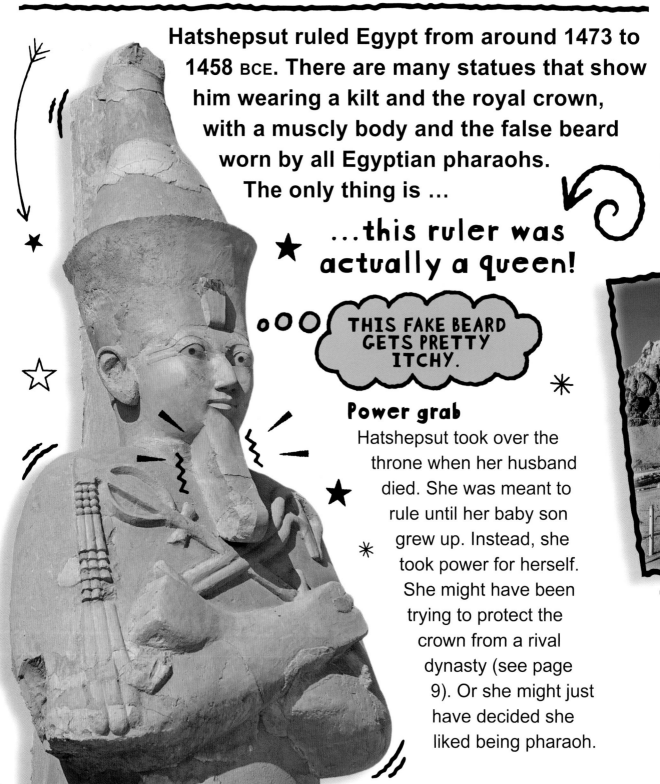

THIS FAKE BEARD GETS PRETTY ITCHY.

Power grab

Hatshepsut took over the throne when her husband died. She was meant to rule until her baby son grew up. Instead, she took power for herself. She might have been trying to protect the crown from a rival dynasty (see page 9). Or she might just have decided she liked being pharaoh.

Who are you calling a girl?

Hatshepsut knew a female ruler would not be popular. There had only been two in the previous 3,000 years, Merneith and Sobekneferu – and Merneith might not even have existed!

Hatshepsut told her subjects that the god Amon-Re had chosen her to rule. She ordered artists and sculptors to show her as a man, although some statues still show her as a woman.

I COMMAND YOU TO BE PHARAOH!

OH, OKAY THEN.

Big builder

One reason Hatshepsut got away with taking the throne is simple: she was a very **GOOD** ruler. She marked her reign by building many grand monuments around her capital city, Thebes.

Hatshepsut's temple at Deir el-Bahari is one of the most famous of all Egyptian buildings.

Keeping the balance

The pharaohs were essential to Egypt. They owned all the land, commanded the army and controlled finances and the law. Above all, they protected Maat – the cosmic sense of balance and justice.

Pharaoh means 'great house', and originally described the royal palace. The pharaohs are usually grouped together in dynasties. A dynasty of rulers all came from the same family.

Why did some of the first pyramids fall down?

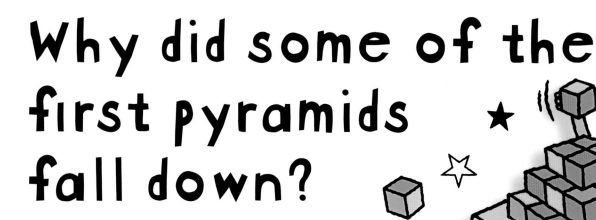

Everyone knows how to build a pyramid from blocks, right? Square at the bottom, pointed at the top, with sides that get narrower as they get higher. How difficult can it be?

Well, more difficult than it looks!

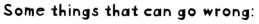

Some things that can go wrong:

Base not square = wonky pyramid
Sides too steep = pyramid too tall
Sides too shallow = pyramid too short
Blocks too heavy = pyramid collapses!

Djoser's tomb

The first pyramid was built around 2650 BCE. It was a tomb (burial chamber) for a pharaoh named Djoser. It began as a traditional tomb called a mastaba – with five more on top in a series of smaller levels. It was a towering 62.5 metres tall. Perhaps Djoser wanted to build a staircase to the sky. Or perhaps he just wanted to show off!

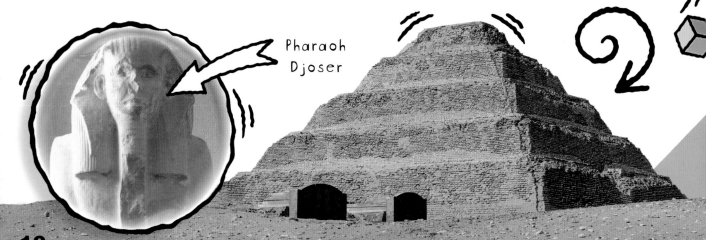

Pharaoh Djoser

Third time lucky!

A few decades later, Sneferu, the first pharaoh of the Fourth Dynasty, decided he also wanted one of these modest monuments.

He ended up building not just one pyramid, but three!

NEARLY...

NEARLY...

NAILED IT!

The first, at Meidum, was a step pyramid like Djoser's. Then someone had the idea of filling in the steps to make four smooth sides. Great idea – poor execution. The sides collapsed.

Sneferu tried again. This time, the sides were too steep. The architects had to change angle. That's why it's called the Bent Pyramid.

Next, Sneferu built the Red Pyramid. It was the first successful smooth-sided pyramid. It gets its name because it's ... red (well, it is today – it was originally covered with white blocks).

There's one big mystery about the Red Pyramid. No-one has ever found Sneferu's burial chamber inside. After all that, did the pharaoh end up in an ordinary tomb?

Total fail!

Building Pyramids

The Egyptians weren't the only ancient people to build pyramids. They were also built by the Babylonians in West Asia, the Kushites in Africa, and by the Maya and Aztecs in the Americas. Why did people want to build tall? Perhaps they believed their gods lived high in the sky.

Why did the Egyptians worship cats?

If you've got a pet, you probably really like it. (Even if it's a snake or a spider.) But you probably don't worship it. No one really worships animals today.

The ancient Egyptians did.

Paw-some Bastet
The Egyptians thought of their gods as animals – or, at least, humans with animal heads. One of the most popular was Bastet, the cat.

Bastet was believed to protect Lower Egypt. She also helped the Sun to ripen crops.

Fortunate felines
Egyptians believed cats were lucky. When a cat died, its owners shaved off their eyebrows as a sign of mourning. If they could afford it, they had their cat turned into a mummy so it could live on in the afterlife.

MEOW!

Yep, you read that right. The cat's body was dried out to preserve it (see pages 14–15) then wrapped in strips of linen and buried in a huge cat cemetery. Other pets that were turned into mummies included dogs, monkeys and birds.

Oh, and whole crocodiles.

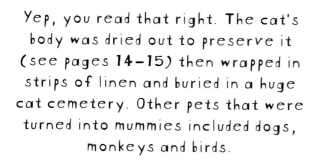

PSST!, NO ONE TOLD ME ABOUT THE CROCODILES!

Cat city

Bastet's temple was at the city of Bubastis. There were more than 300,000 mummified cats buried there. Many cats were also sacrificed there as gifts to Bastet.

HERE'S TO YOU WHISKERS. HIC!

Every year, Bubastis held a festival for Bastet. About 700,000 worshippers came to make sacrifices and eat and drink — especially drink.

Top gods!

The Egyptians had many animal gods. These are just some of the most important:

Sekhmet the lion – goddess of war

Anubis the jackal – god of the dead

Horus the falcon – god of kingship and the sky

Sobek the crocodile – god of the Nile

What happened to the pharaoh's brain?

From the 16th century, there were so many mummies in Egypt that they were ground up to make a popular shade of paint called mummy brown.

✳ FACT!

Obviously, that wasn't the original intention!
Egyptians turned people (and animals) into mummies to
keep their bodies in good shape for the afterlife.

How to make a mummy

Making a mummy was a long process. You needed a long time.
And a strong stomach. (Don't try this at home!)

① Wash the body.

② Cut it open and remove the lungs, liver, stomach and intestines. Keep them to one side. (Leave the heart where it is. It's needed later.)

Tools

③ Push a long probe up the nose, and move it around to mash up the brain. Then pull the mess back out through the nose!

④ Stuff the body with straw, grass or dry mud to help keep its shape. Pack the body and organs in natron, a special salt. Leave for forty days to dry out.

⑤ Put each of the organs in its own canopic jar.

WHAT HAVE YOU GOT? · LIVER! · YUK! · YUM!

14

6 Add glass eyes so that the mummy can see in the afterlife.

7 Wrap the body in linen bandages. Include charms between the bandages to protect the dead person from evil.

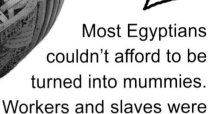
Bandage

Ankh charm

Scarab beetle charm

I WAS VERY IMPORTANT YOU KNOW!

8 Bury the body in a coffin.

Most Egyptians couldn't afford to be turned into mummies. Workers and slaves were just put into a hole in the ground.

Which way to paradise?

Most mummies were buried in mastabas. These tombs were sometimes painted with spells or contained scrolls. The scrolls gave directions to the afterlife in case the dead person was confused or had forgotten where they had to go.

In the balance!

The heart was left inside a mummy because it had to be weighed.

If your heart was lighter than a feather, hey presto — you'd lived a good life, and you were off to the Field of Reeds, or paradise. If it was heavier... uh-oh. That meant endless torment in the Underworld ...

The god Osiris ran the ceremony of weighing the heart.

Was the Great Pyramid a giant booby trap?

Khufu was not a modest pharaoh. His Great Pyramid at Giza wasn't just the tallest pyramid in Egypt. It was the tallest building anywhere for 38 centuries!

As well as wanting to be remembered, Khufu wanted to be undisturbed. Robbers broke into lots of Egyptian tombs because people were buried with valuable possessions to take with them to the afterlife.

Disguising the tomb

Khufu's architects made it difficult for anyone to break into his pyramid.

① A tunnel sloped down from a hidden entrance into the rock beneath the pyramid.

② The tunnel reached a burial chamber – but it was a decoy. To reach the real burial chamber, you had to go **UP**. The entrance to the upward passage was hidden in the ceiling of the downward tunnel.

③ The upward passage sloped up past another chamber. **Empty!**

④ Eventually, the passage flattened out, reaching the real burial chamber.

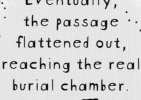

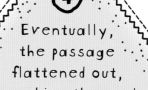

Pharaoh Khufu

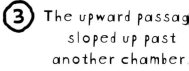

Where's Khufu?

The burial chamber was guarded by stones that slid down in grooves to block the entrance.

Were the blocks intended to trap robbers who got inside the tomb?

Probably not, but we'll never know. The blocks have disappeared.

And so has Khufu.

The burial chamber holds a broken stone sarcophagus and … nothing else. Maybe the tomb was robbed after all.

In the 9th century, an Islamic ruler was said to have broken into the tomb and found great stores of gold.

Grave robots

The Great Pyramid has 23 million blocks — lots of room for secrets! We know it holds small tunnels that might be for ventilation, and other tunnels that lead to closed doors. There might be other chambers still to find. Archaeologists are exploring with robots. But there's an awful lot of pyramid to explore.

How did an old stone reveal the secrets of ancient Egypt?

Ancient Egyptian monuments are covered with picture writing that is carved into stone or painted on walls. For centuries, though, no one had any idea what it said.

FRUSTRATING!

Scribe

Sacred symbols

The symbols are called hieroglyphs, which is Greek for 'sacred writing', because they were used for religious purposes. Scribes, the officials who kept records in Egypt, had to learn about 700 different hieroglyphs.

Most Egyptians couldn't read or write. Not even the pharaohs.

ALLO ALLO!

An important find

In 1799, French soldiers invaded Egypt. While they were building a fort in a place called Rosetta, one of them found a buried piece of a stone tablet. The stone was carved with three different sorts of writing.

One of the scripts was hieroglyphs. Another was demotic, a simpler form of Egyptian writing (it took ages to write in hieroglyphs). The third was ancient Greek.

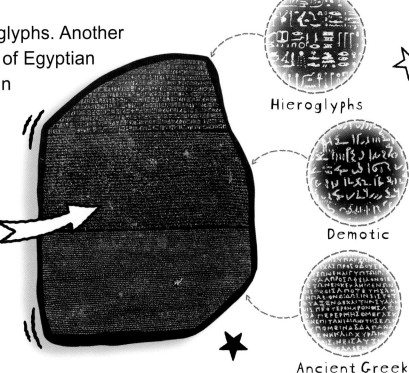

Hieroglyphs

Demotic

Ancient Greek

The Rosetta Stone, as it became known, was the key to the code. The three scripts contained the same passage of text. (Lucky!) Lots of people could still read ancient Greek.

Cracking the code

Two men, Thomas Young and Jean-Paul Champollion, spent years comparing the three texts. Eventually, Champollion made a breakthrough. He realised that while some hieroglyphs stood for words, they could also stand for sounds as part of words.

That complicated things, but it was the clue scholars needed. They slowly began to decipher the hieroglyphs — and learn more about the secrets of ancient Egypt.

Scribe scribble!

TRANSLATION: I MUST NOT MAKE SPELLING MISTAKES. I MUST NOT MAKE SPELLING MISTAKES. I MUST NOT...

YAWN!

Being a scribe was such an important job that it was handed down from father to son. Boys spent four or five years at a special school to learn hieroglyphs, and a faster way of writing called hieratic. They practised on stone or on paper made from papyrus until they got the symbols right.

Did Tutankhamun die in a traffic accident?

HEY!

Tutankhamun wasn't much of a pharaoh. He took the throne aged eight or nine and ruled for about ten years. In fact, the most famous thing about him is about his death!

World famous mummy

Tutankhamun was buried in a tomb that stayed hidden for more than 3,200 years – until the archaeologist Howard Carter opened it in November 1922.

Overnight, Tutankhamun became the most famous ancient Egyptian in the world.

★ Tutankhamun was buried inside three coffins inside a stone sarcophagus. The innermost coffin was solid gold.

Tomb of treasures

The boy-king was buried with so many belongings that it took ten years to list all 5,398 objects. They included four chariots, 80 vases, 26 jars of wine, 35 model boats and two trumpets!

Covering the mummy's face was a gold mask showing Tutankhamun in his royal headdress.

CSI Pharaoh Tut

What everyone wants to know is:

Why did Tutankhamun die so young?

The pharaoh's skeleton shows that he suffered from lots of diseases. Injuries to his chest and leg suggest he died from a collision. Perhaps he was thrown from a chariot. Another theory is that he was attacked by a hippopotamus.

HELP!

Yet another is that he was murdered by a blow to the head. The prime suspect was the chief priest, Ay. He ruled Egypt while Tutankhamun was young. After the king died, Ay took the throne for himself.

Suspicious!

Pharaoh's curse

Be afraid. Be very afraid!

Some people claim Egyptian tombs were protected by spells. Four months after Tutankhamun's tomb was opened, a man who helped fund the operation died from an infected mosquito bite. Some people were convinced he was the victim of a curse.

How did the Egyptians break their teeth?

Mummification was all about keeping the Egyptians looking their best. There was only one problem: the Egyptians had **TERRIBLE** teeth.

SO RUDE!

The ancient Egyptians may have reattached lost teeth to their gums with wire. Ouch!

Virtually everyone's teeth were broken or ground right down. (There's a reason Egyptians had some of the first dentists. They must have had a **LOT** of toothaches.)

True grit!

The reason was right in front of the Egyptians when they ate. **Bread**. Flatbread made from barley was part of nearly every meal. It was full of grit and sand from the stones used to grind the flour. It didn't exactly melt in the mouth...

...and it wore out the teeth!

Bread wasn't the only thing that gave dentists nightmares. Sugary honey and dates also caused tooth decay.

What's to eat?

Apart from bread, other staple food included perch from the Nile. Only the wealthy could afford to eat much meat: they ate poultry, goat and lamb. Beef was so valuable that a man's wealth was measured in how many cows he owned. Both fish and meat were preserved by being covered in salt.

Also on the menu:

Palm-tree fruit

Sycamore figs

Pomegranates

Ox heart

Leeks

Calf's head

Onions

Lentils

Most of the time, it was far too hot to work in a kitchen. Most food was cooked outdoors, over huge fires.

PHEW, THIRSTY WORK!

And drink?

To drink, there was wine or beer. Egyptian beer was made by mashing up loaves of bread made from barley. It was so thick it was like soup. It had to be drunk through a strainer. Nice!

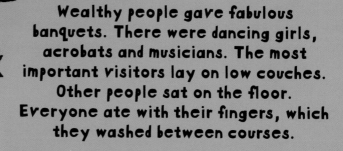

Party time!

Wealthy people gave fabulous banquets. There were dancing girls, acrobats and musicians. The most important visitors lay on low couches. Other people sat on the floor. Everyone ate with their fingers, which they washed between courses.

What gave Nefertiti black eyes?

The most famous sculpture of Queen Nefertiti has thick black lines painted around her eyes. In fact, virtually every image of an ancient Egyptian has huge black eyes.

The eyes have it!

Egyptians of both sexes coloured their upper eyelids with black powder and their lower eyelids with green. They made their eyes almond-shaped, like the eye of the falcon god, Horus. They may have thought this protected them against magic.

Making make-up

The powder was made by grinding up minerals called kohl (black) and malachite (green). Iron ores made red powder that was mixed with animal fat, then rubbed on the cheeks and lips.

Sounds, um... colourful...

LOOKING GOOD!

People ground up their make-up on flat slate tablets. They checked how they looked in mirrors of polished bronze or copper.

Hair-raising stories

Think of those pictures of Egyptians again.
Notice how their hair is all exactly the same?

Wigs!

Wealthy Egyptians shaved their heads, then wore wigs made of human hair. Not-so-wealthy Egyptians shaved their heads, then wore wigs made of wool or even grass. Poor Egyptians shaved their heads, then sold their hair to wealthy Egyptians.

PHEEEEW!

Wigs were cooler than real hair and prevented head lice. They were held in place with wax. On special occasions, people wore cones of animal fat on top of their wigs that slowly melted. This gave off an attractive scent.

(Well, maybe not that attractive.)

Hot fashion!

Egypt's weather was usually very hot, so clothes were light and cool. Men wore a skirt-like kilt, and women wore long shift dresses. Clothes were woven from linen, made from the fibres of flax.

Why was Cleopatra rolled up in a carpet?

The Egyptian queen Cleopatra was famous for her beauty. Two of the most powerful men in the world fell madly in love with her.

Cleopatra

JC

MA

IT'S MINE!

ISN'T!

Troubled times

Cleopatra was from the Greek Ptolemy family who had ruled Egypt for 300 years. But now Rome was taking Egypt's lands; worse still, Egypt was suffering from a famine. Not only that, Cleopatra had to share the throne with her little brother, Ptolemy XIII.

A powerful ally

Cleopatra needed an ally. Luckily enough, the most powerful man in the world visited Egypt in 48 BCE: Julius Caesar, ruler of Rome. Cleopatra had to meet him without Ptolemy stopping her.

SURPRISE!

Cleopatra put on her best clothes and had herself rolled up in a carpet that was carried to Caesar's room.

When Cleopatra rolled out of the carpet, Caesar was bowled over. Perhaps literally. Not only did he make an alliance with Cleopatra to get her throne back, he also became her partner. They later had a son, Caesarion.

Cleopatra (left) and Caesarion

Change of plan

Cleopatra and her son were in Rome when Caesar was assassinated there in 44 BCE. Time for a quick getaway!

One of Rome's new rulers, Mark Antony, took charge of Egypt. Cleopatra made an impression on him, too. This time, she presented herself to Mark Antony dressed as a goddess beneath a gilded canopy floating on a golden barge. Again, they fell in love and eventually got married.

A coin showing Mark Antony

Not-so-happy ending

Later, Mark Antony and Cleopatra went to war against Rome to protect Egypt.

Big mistake.

After they were defeated, Mark Antony stabbed himself to death, while Cleopatra let a deadly poisonous snake bite her. In 30 BCE Egypt became a province of the Roman Empire and the ancient Egyptian civilisation came to an end after more than 3,500 years.

Quick-fire questions

What was fake about the most famous Egyptian queen?

Well, Cleopatra wasn't actually Egyptian. Even though she was born in Egypt, she belonged to the Ptolemaic dynasty who took control of Egypt in 323 BCE. They were from Macedonia, then part of Greece. In order to get their Egyptian subjects to accept their rule, they took on the role of Egyptian pharaohs.

I'M AN EGYPTIAN, HONEST!

How did Egyptian workers hold the first strike?

NO WORK WITHOUT PAY!

NO BREAD, NO BRICKS!

Building pyramids or temples took so long that craftsmen and builders lived in special villages at the site. The government paid them and provided their supplies. When the workers of Deir el-Medina did not receive their rations, they went on strike – probably the first strike anywhere, ever. They sat down in one of the temples they had built and refused to leave until the rations arrived.

What did the Egyptians do to have fun?

Wealthy Egyptians had lots of spare time. One way they filled it was with board games such as Senet and Aseb. The players threw knuckle bones as a kind of dice that told them how many spaces to move their counters. The games weren't just for fun. They relied on chance, which reminded the Egyptians that their lives were in the control of the gods.

What is a sphinx?

The Egyptians carved sculptures of lions with the wrong heads. Some had the heads of rams, and others of humans. These creatures were called sphinxes, and were thought to protect humans. The most famous sphinx, the Great Sphinx of Giza, has the body of a lion and the head of a human. It guards the Great Pyramid of Khufu and may have the face of the pharaoh Khufu himself.

Great Sphinx of Giza

Glossary

Afterlife The place where people's souls are believed to live on after their death.

Alliance An association between countries that helps them both.

Architect A person who designs buildings.

Archaeologist A person who studies the physical remains of the past.

Assassinated Murdered for a political reason

Chariot A two-wheeled horse-drawn vehicle with a flat platform for a driver and passengers.

Civilisation A society, or group, of people who have advanced social and cultural structures.

Cosmic Relating to the universe.

Curse A magic spell that will bring harm to someone as a punishment.

Decoy A trick version of something used to distract attention from the real thing.

Delta A triangular area with many water channels formed where a river meets the sea.

Fertile Land that is fertile can produce many crops.

Flax A plant whose fibres are used to make linen cloth.

Intermediate Occurring between two things in time.

Intestines The internal digestive organs.

Irrigation Using water for growing crops.

Islamic Belonging or relating to the religion of Islam.

Mastaba A room-shaped tomb built of stone.

Mourning An expression of sorrow when someone dies.

Mummy A dead body preserved by being dried and wrapped in linen.

Nutrients Chemicals that provide energy for plants or animals.

Palette A flat object used for mixing paints or make-up.

Papyrus A paper-like substance made from the papyrus reed.

Pharaoh The name given to rulers of ancient Egypt.

Pyramid A four-sided structure that rises to a point.

Sarcophagus A stone coffin.

Scroll A long roll of paper or other material for writing on.

Mini timeline

3150 BCE
Upper and Lower Egypt are united, creating a single kingdom.

2650 BCE
Pharaoh Djoser builds the first pyramid.

1550 BCE
The New Kingdom begins, marking the height of Egypt's power.

1473 BCE
Hatshepsut takes the Egyptian throne and rules as a man.

323 BCE
The Ptolemaic dynasty of Greece takes over Egypt.

30 BCE
A Roman army defeats Cleopatra and Egypt becomes part of the Roman Empire.

Further reading

Websites

www.natgeokids.com/uk/discover/history/egypt/ten-facts-about-ancient-egypt/

Learn ten fascinating facts about the ancient Egyptians.

www.bbc.co.uk/bitesize/topics/zg87xnb

This page has an index of articles and videos about ancient Egypt on the BBC Bitesize site.

www.dkfindout.com/uk/history/ancient-egypt/

This interactive map of Egypt has links to different places and aspects of Egyptian life.

www.historyforkids.net/rosetta-stone.html

This page has an explanation of the Rosetta Stone and why it is so important for understanding ancient Egypt.

Books

Black History: African Empires
by Dan Lyndon-Cohen (Franklin Watts, 2020)

The Genius of The Ancient Egyptians
by Sonya Newland (Franklin Watts, 2020)

History in Infographics: Ancient Egyptians
by Jon Richards (Wayland, 2018)

Great Empires: The Egyptian Empire
by Ellis Roxburgh (Wayland, 2015)

Every effort has been made by the Publishers to ensure that the websites in this book are suitable for children, that they are of the highest educational value, and that they contain no inappropriate or offensive material. However, because of the nature of the Internet, it is impossible to guarantee that the contents of these sites will not be altered. We strongly advise that internet access is supervised by a responsible adult.

Index